About this Book

We created **Love–U–Grams** because we know how important it is for you to connect with the kids in your life! Time, distance, school, and soccer (and football and gymnastics and karate and...) keep us apart from these little people we love so much... So, we've created fun ways to keep us close at heart!

Love-U-Grams feature three types of "grams":

Postcards – Who doesn't love getting mail? Whether you wish to send a hug or say hello from a business trip, our postcards deliver love to a special girl's or boy's mailbox.

Lunch Notes – Meant to be tucked into a lunchbox, backpack, gym bag or under a pillow, these little notes are sure to make a kid feel loved and appreciated.

Kid Coupons – The littlest things make a kid's day... being able to pick the movie or enjoying a "mom and me" round of mini golf. Hand these coupons out with care when you really want to see a smile!

Love–U–Grams

This book is part of the **I Love You So...** product collection,
written and illustrated by Marianne Richmond.

©2005 by Marianne Richmond Studios, Inc.

Marianne Richmond Studios, Inc.
420 N. 5th Street, Suite 840
Minneapolis, MN 55401
www.mariannerichmond.com

ISBN 1-58209-526-4
This printing manufactured exclusively for Books are Fun.

Text and illustrations by Marianne Richmond

Book design by Meg Anderson

Printed in China

Second Printing

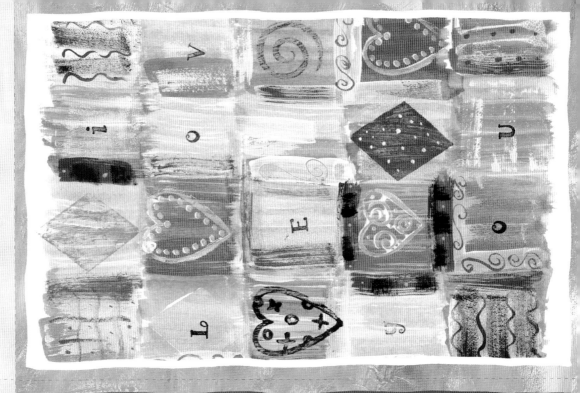

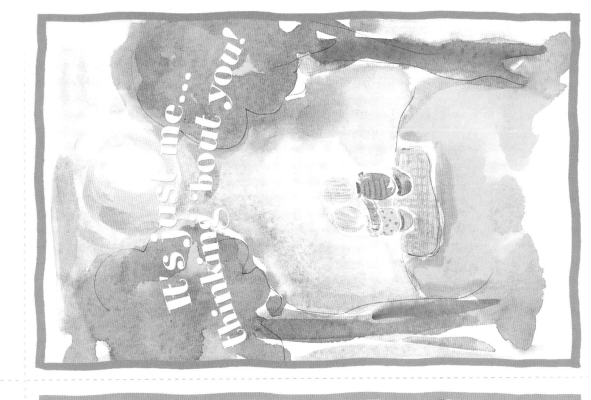

I think the world of you!

You're the BEST!

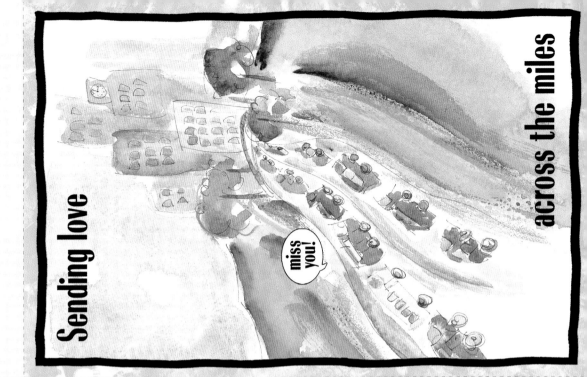

Hope you're having a great day!

I'm thinking about you today!

You are loved!

Hooray for you!

Do you know
you're incredible?

Remember:
I love
you!

What's the
best part
about today?

Great job on your homework!

Make your teacher laugh...

Sending a hug

I think the world of you!

I love you!

I LOVE YOU

chuckle   snicker

snort   guffaw

howl   Make someone laugh today   chortle

roar

cackle   giggle   heehaw

Make someone laugh today

Kid Coupons

This coupon is good for a trip to the **Toy Store**

This coupon is good for **One extra serving Of dessert** your choice!

This coupon is good for one trip to the park

This coupon is good for a trip to a clothing store

(for an accessory under $10)

This coupon is good for renting a movie of your choice from the video store

This coupon is good
for one trip to the
bookstore or library

This coupon is good for a trip to the

Toy
Store

for a toy under $10

This coupon is good
for one game of

miniature golf

This coupon is good for
staying up
one hour
past your
bedtime

This coupon is good for

Family Game Night

You pick the game!

This coupon is good for

Family Game Night

You pick the game!

USE THIS COUPON TO GO OUT FOR ICE CREAM

This coupon is good for a trip to the zoo

This coupon is
good for one
dad-and-me
activity
(your choice)

This coupon is
good for one
mom-and-me
activity
(your choice)

Use this coupon to eat lunch while watching tv

This coupon is good for one treat at the grocery store checkout

Use this coupon
to eat breakfast
for dinner

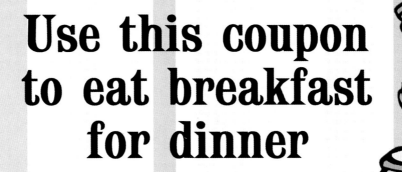

Use this coupon
to order pizza
for dinner

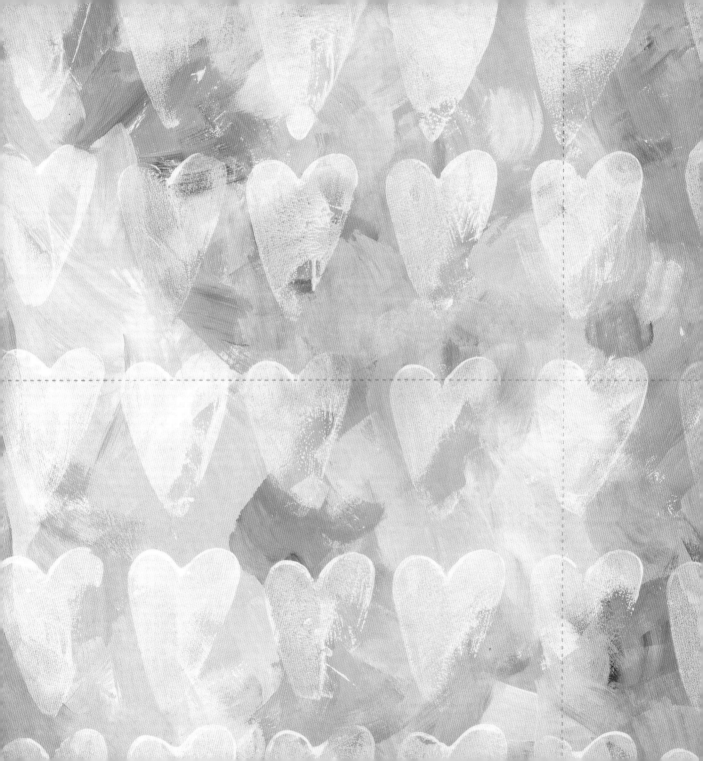